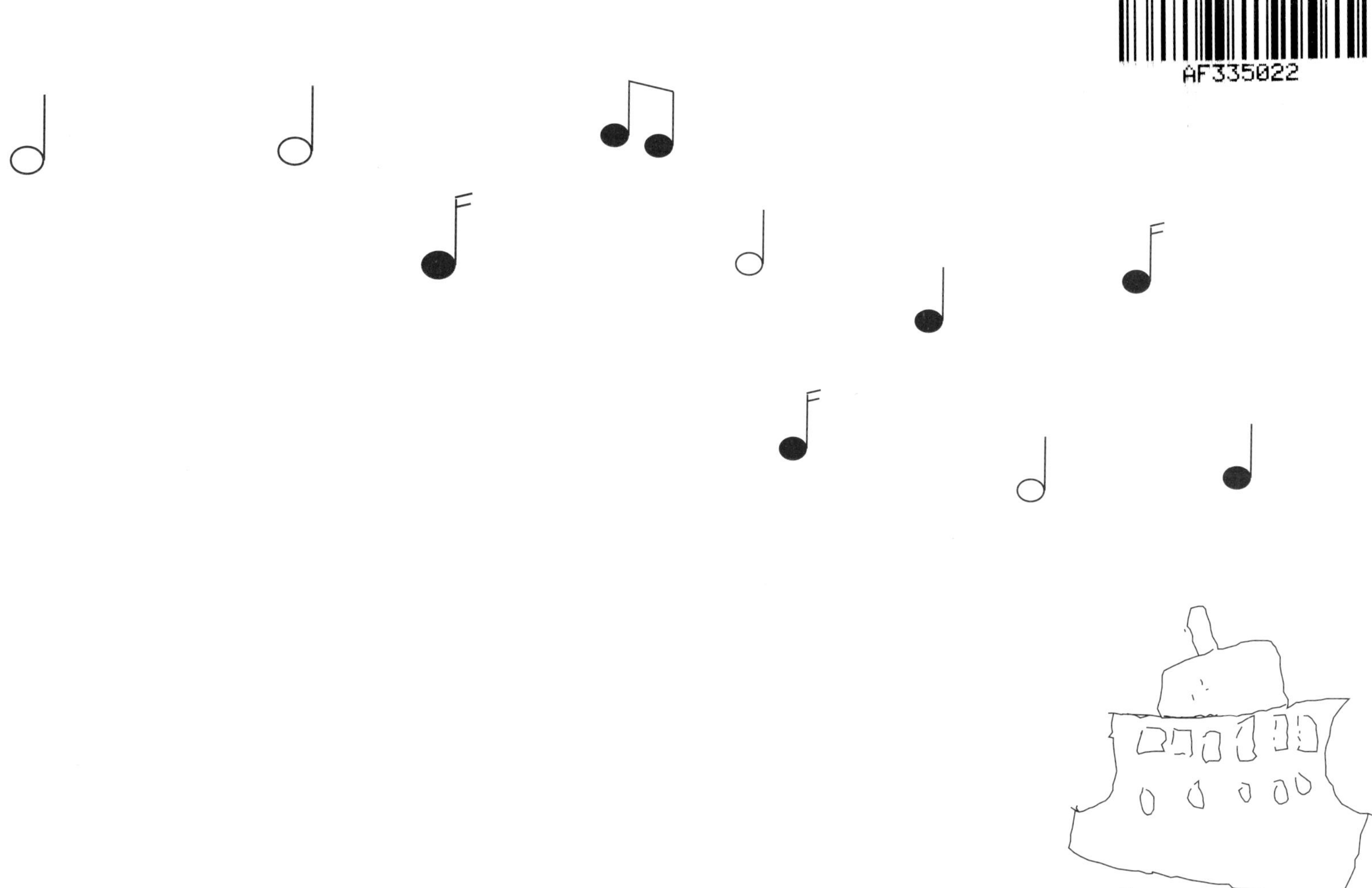

Published by
**Raindrop Press**
PO Box 76
Port Townsend, WA 98368
solmaker@olympus.net



ISBN: 0-9638698-6-8

To order this book
Contact:
Harmony Preschool
728 Adams Street
Port Townsend, WA 98368
360.385.4769

# THE FERRYBOAT
# *I WONDER*

by Keith Jackson

Photographs by Nick Reid

Raindrop Press

Port Townsend, Washington

Dedicated to...

All of the Talented Parents
and
Children of *Harmony Preschool*

Spencer Jackson,  Joey Morello, Phoebe Reid, Dakota Sandoval-Gay, Alia Stevens, Mariah Vane


Special thanks to David Michael for the fog photograph

This is a story about a ferryboat named *I Wonder*. It is a rather unusual name for a ferryboat, but people used to say, "I wonder what makes that ferryboat run?"

I WONDER

The captain's name is Captain Lollypop.  He carries lollypops in all of his pockets and hands them out to everyone as they board his ferry.

The unusual thing about this ferryboat is that it does not run on coal or oil or gasoline. Captain Lollypop decided to make it run on music! He removed the oil tanks and invented a music drinking carburetor. He connected a huge music box to it,  which made the most beautiful sound. The music flowed into the carburetor, making the engine go chunk, chunk, chunk. Then it went right up the smoke stack where you could see the musical notes fly out like small lively birds.

The *I Wonder* leaves Port Townsend every Wednesday morning and goes to a place called Mysterious Island. It leaves on that day because the island is only there on Wednesdays. The island appears in the morning and then disappears into the fog about dinner time.  It is a nice little island. It has wonderful beaches with lots of driftwood and picnic tables where you can eat your lunch.  The picnic area is very clean because everyone picks up his or her own litter.  The *I Wonder* returns to Port Townsend in the afternoon several hours before Mysterious Island begins to disappear.

No one knows what would happen if Captain Lollypop forgot to look at his watch, and the island disappeared while they were still there...

$W$ell... this one particular Wednesday there were many children who were going to Mysterious Island for a picnic.  Among them were six students from Harmony Preschool.  This is a school where little kids learn to play the violin.  They boarded the magic ferryboat, and the captain gave them each a lollypop.

When they were halfway to Mysterious Island, there was a bit of a mishap. Captain Lollypop, being a very neat and careful sailor, kept everything clean and ship-shape. There he was leaning over his music box, polishing it to a bright shine, when *OOPS*, some lollypops fell into the gears of the music box and got stuck.

The music stopped!

M·A·M·O·D

At that very moment, they were approaching a place called Point Teeth.  This was a jagged group of rocks that looked rather like sharp teeth, and it could be very dangerous!  The captain explained to the boys and girls,  "We have a problem.  The engine requires music, and my music box is broken. I see that we have students here from Harmony Preschool, and I see that they have brought their violins." He asked their teacher, Miss Kerry, "Do you think that your students would play their violins for me and help make the boat go?"

"I  hope so," she said.

Miss Kerry asked, "Well, how about it students?"

"Yes! Yes!" they all cried.

"Okay, let's go down to the engine room!" urged the captain.  The students went below with their violins, and they all stood around the engine and played the most beautiful music.  The engine went kachunk, kachunk, kachunk, and then it started running smoothly. They pulled away from Point Teeth just in the nick of time.

ENGINE ROOM

The *I Wonder* then proceeded on to Mysterious Island where the children got off and had a delightful picnic.

Captain Lollypop stayed on board and tried to pull  the lollypops out of the music box, but he could not do it.  They were very sticky and firmly wedged in the gears.

Finally, when everyone came back on board, he had to say to the children from Harmony, "Children, children, we need to leave quickly because the island will soon disappear. My music box is still not working. Do you think that you could play us home to Port Townsend?"

The children all said, "Yes! Yes! Yes!" because they were very enthusiastic violinists.

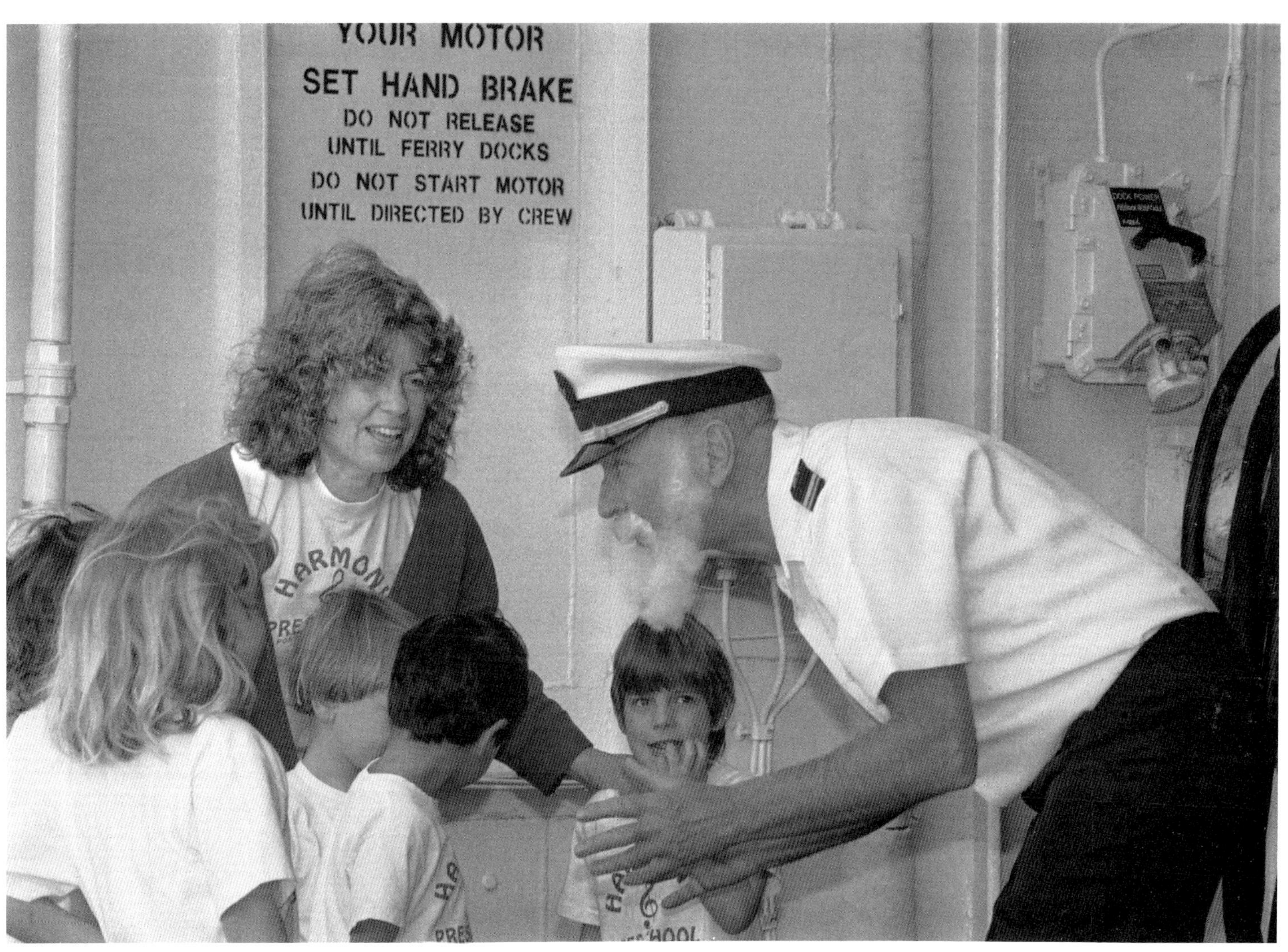
YOUR MOTOR
SET HAND BRAKE
DO NOT RELEASE
UNTIL FERRY DOCKS
DO NOT START MOTOR
UNTIL DIRECTED BY CREW

The children took turns playing their pieces.  Sometimes they played together and sometimes individually, and the engine drank up all of the music.

They played and the ferryboat chugged happily all the way back to Port Townsend.

The End